God's Children

PERTTI PIETARINEN

Copyright © 2018 Pertti Pietarinen
All rights reserved.

No part of this publication may be reproduced, stored in a retrieval system or transmitted, in any form or by any means, digital, mechanical, photo-copying, recording or otherwise, without the prior consent of the copyright owner.
For permission requests, write to perttipietarinen@hotmail.com.

Publisher: Papan Publishing

ISBN-13: 978-952-7304-00-6

DEDICATION

To All Children In The World

Read other books from Pertti Pietarinen:
Lucy The Cat: ISBN 978-1494444136, 2014
http://www.amazon.com/dp/B00IARLDCY

God's Children: ISBN 978-9527304006, 2018

Kingdom of God: ISBN 978-9527304044, 2018

Lucy The Cat: Little Brother: ISBN 978-1500770396, 2014
http://www.amazon.com/dp/B00MQI99N8

Lucy The Cat Play With Me: ISBN 978-1505607000, 2015
http://www.amazon.com/dp/B00STTT01Y

Lucy The Cat And Little Kittens: ISBN 978-1515385288, 2015
http://www.amazon.com/dp/B014FPTOM0

Lucy The Cat Christmas: ISBN 978-1517153700, 2015
https://www.amazon.com//dp/B0178BBRCS

Lucy The Cat Sushi Time: ISBN 978-1532867163, 2016
https://www.amazon.com/dp/B01FG17V4K

Lucy The Cat Beauty And The Feast: ISBN 978- 1539533993, 2017
https://www.amazon.com/dp/1539533999

Lucy The Cat in Tokyo: ISBN 978-1974145355, 2017
https://www.amazon.com/dp/1547269308

Lucy The Cat in Tokyo 2: ISBN 978-1977655752, 2018
https://www.amazon.com/dp/1977655750

Learn more:
http://www.pietarinen.org
https://www.facebook.com/lucythecat
https://www.facebook.com/GodsChildrenBook

**My dear friend, you are surrounded by love.
Your mom and dad surely love you. You are so dear to them.**

And there is your heavenly Father, who loves you. God is the love.

**God loves you, because He created you
and everyone as His own Image.
Isn't that great?**

**God has created everything in this world.
He has created the whole Universe very, very long time ago.**

When God created people he granted us the nicest place to live in, the paradise. It was so beautiful, that I am not able to describe it.

It was full of nice and gentle animals, and it was filled with trees and most beautiful flowers. Please close your eyes and try to imagine the most wonderful flowers.

But, the first people did some wrong things against God's will and therefore they had to leave the paradise. After that we have never been able to find the way back to the paradise.

But God has still given us lovely flowers. So we can admire and dream of paradise. Do you love flowers? I do.

God's Children

God loves us more than anything else.
He loves so much that he gave His only Son, Jesus Christ.
God so loved the world he gave His only begotten Son, that whosoever believes in Him should not perish, but have everlasting life.

**Isn't that wonderful?
We have our best friend in Jesus.
He is our Savior.**

Jesus is really your Friend. He loves every child.

He once said to His followers:
"Let the children come to me, and do not keep them away, for of such is the kingdom of heaven. Truly I say to you, Whoever does not put himself under the kingdom of God like a little child, will not come into it at all."

Jesus loves every child and tells us:
"See that you do not despise one of these little ones. For I tell you that in heaven their angels always see the face of my Father who is in heaven."

Because God loves children, He has assigned a guardian angel to everyone to protect for all kind of dangers.

You can feel safe, because you have your own guardian angel walking by your side. Your angel is so white and beautiful. Have you seen her?

**When you sleep thru the night,
your guardian angel will stay by your side.**

God loves you and you should love Him, too.

Jesus said:
Have love for the Lord your God with all your heart and with all your soul and with all your strength and with all your mind; and for your neighbor as for yourself.

**The Lord takes care of you every day and everywhere.
Even if you feel sad you can pray the Lord.
And He will comfort you!**

**God is our refuge and strength, He will help us in all our troubles.
He is our comfort and joy.**

**Everything is possible to God, nothing is impossible to Him.
He is our almighty Heavenly Father.**

Jesus tells us: "Remain in me, and I will remain in you."

**This is the day
the Lord has made.
Let us rejoice and be glad in it.**

People look at the outsider of a person, but the Lord looks at the heart.

**And the peace of God,
which passes all understanding,
shall keep your hearts and minds through Christ Jesus.**

**Rejoice!
Rejoice, because your names are written in heaven!**

Thank you, Lord, for loving me and keeping me safe.

Thank you, Lord, for creating this wonderful world.

Dear Jesus, help me to take care of this wonderful world.

Thank you, Lord, for everything.

**Jesus loves me! He will stay
Close beside me all the way!**

God's Children

www.ingramcontent.com/pod-product-compliance
Lightning Source LLC
Chambersburg PA
CBHW062025050526
44107CB00105B/914